COM~ CHAM~ ~X- MONT-BLANC TRAVEL GUIDE

BY

JOHN MILLER

TABLE OF CONTENT

INTRODUCTION

History of Chamonix

Chamonix-Mont-Blanc, commonly known as Chamonix, is a renowned alpine resort town located in the Haute-Savoie region of the French Alps. Its history is closely intertwined with the development of mountaineering and winter sports.

Chamonix gained prominence in the 18th century when the first explorers and scientists, including Horace-Bénédict de Saussure, began to visit the region to study its natural beauty. However, it wasn't until 1741 that two Englishmen, William Windham and Richard Pococke, embarked on a tour of the Mont Blanc Massif, sparking interest in the challenging ascent of Mont Blanc.

In 1786, Jacques Balmat and Michel Paccard made history by becoming the first climbers to successfully reach the summit of Mont Blanc, marking the birth of modern mountaineering. This achievement catapulted Chamonix into the international spotlight.

In the 19th century, Chamonix continued to attract adventurers and mountaineers, becoming a hub for alpinism. The town's popularity grew with the construction of the Mer de Glace railway in the early 20th century, making the region more accessible to tourists.

Today, Chamonix is celebrated not only for its mountaineering history but also for its world-class skiing, snowboarding, and outdoor activities, making it a year-round destination for those seeking both adventure and natural beauty in the heart of the Alps.

CHAPTER ONE

Chamonix Travel Guide Itinerary

Chamonix-Mont-Blanc, nestled in the French Alps, is a dream destination for outdoor enthusiasts, adventure seekers, and nature lovers. With its stunning mountain landscapes, charming alpine villages, and a wealth of activities, Chamonix offers an unforgettable experience year-round.

Here's a travel guide itinerary to help you make the most of your visit:

Day 1: Arrival in Chamonix

Morning: Arrive in Chamonix and settle into your accommodation. Take in the breathtaking views of Mont Blanc.

Afternoon: Stroll through Chamonix town, explore boutique shops, and savor French cuisine at a local restaurant.

Evening: Relax and prepare for your upcoming adventures.

Day 2: Outdoor Exploration

Morning: Start your day with a cable car ride to Aiguille du Midi for panoramic views of the Alps.

Afternoon: Hike around the Mer de Glace glacier or visit the Ice Cave.

Evening: Enjoy dinner in one of Chamonix's many restaurants.

Day 3: Chamonix Adventures

Morning: Take the Montenvers Railway to see the Mer de Glace glacier up close.

Afternoon: Thrill-seekers can go paragliding, while others can explore the charming town of Les Houches.

Evening: Relax at a local spa or enjoy a leisurely dinner.

Day 4: Alpine Excursions

Morning: Visit the nearby town of Annecy, known as the "Venice of the Alps," for its stunning canals and old town.

Afternoon: Return to Chamonix and explore more of the town's culture and history.

Evening: Dine at a mountain restaurant for a taste of Savoyard cuisine.

Day 5: Outdoor Activities

Morning: Embark on a guided mountain biking or hiking adventure in the Chamonix Valley.

Afternoon: Try your hand at rock climbing or visit the Alpine Museum for insights into the region's mountaineering history.

Evening: Wrap up your day with a fondue dinner.

Day 6: Departure

Morning: Before leaving, take one last look at the stunning landscapes and perhaps purchase some souvenirs.

Afternoon: Depart from Chamonix with incredible memories and a deep appreciation for the natural beauty of the French Alps.

Why Choose Chamonix for Vacation?

Chamonix, nestled in the heart of the French Alps, stands as a premier destination for those seeking a truly remarkable mountain experience. Here are some compelling reasons why you should choose Chamonix for your next adventure:

Spectacular Alpine Scenery: Chamonix boasts some of the most awe-inspiring mountain vistas in the world, including the iconic Mont Blanc. The dramatic peaks, glaciers, and valleys create an unparalleled backdrop for outdoor enthusiasts and photographers.

World-Class Skiing: Known as the "Capital of Extreme Skiing," Chamonix offers access to a vast ski area with challenging terrain for advanced skiers and snowboarders, as well as plenty of beginner-friendly slopes.

Year-Round Activities: Beyond skiing and snowboarding, Chamonix offers a plethora of activities, such as hiking, mountain biking, paragliding, and rock climbing. In the summer, the region transforms into a paradise for outdoor adventurers.

Rich History and Culture: Chamonix has a charming alpine village atmosphere with cozy cafes, restaurants serving delectable Savoyard cuisine, and a vibrant cultural scene. Explore the town's history through its museums and architecture.

Adventure Hub: It serves as a gateway to the pristine wilderness of the Mont Blanc Massif, making it a hub for mountaineers and hikers seeking to conquer the highest peak in Western Europe.

Wellness and Relaxation: Chamonix offers numerous spas and wellness centers where you can unwind after an action-packed day in the mountains.

Accessibility: Located just an hour from Geneva Airport, Chamonix is easily accessible for international travelers, making it a convenient destination for a short getaway or an extended stay.

Year-Round Beauty: Chamonix's allure doesn't fade with the seasons. Whether you visit in winter, spring, summer, or fall, you'll be captivated by its ever-changing beauty.

Environmental Consciousness: Chamonix is committed to sustainable tourism, actively promoting eco-friendly practices to preserve its natural beauty for generations to come.

Chamonix offers a perfect blend of natural grandeur, adrenaline-pumping activities, cultural richness, and relaxation, making it an exceptional choice for anyone seeking an unforgettable mountain adventure.

Best Time to Visit

Winter (December to February):

Winter is the prime season for skiers and snowboarders. Chamonix boasts excellent skiing conditions, with a plethora of slopes and resorts.

The town comes alive with a festive atmosphere, making it a great time for apres-ski activities and enjoying cozy evenings by the fireplace.

Be prepared for cold temperatures and heavy snowfall, so make sure to pack accordingly.

Spring (March to May): Spring in Chamonix offers milder weather and longer days, making it an ideal time for those who enjoy both winter and spring activities.

Skiing is still possible in the higher altitudes, and hiking trails start to emerge as the snow melts.

It's a quieter period, perfect for those seeking a more peaceful experience.

Summer (June to August):

Summer is the time for outdoor enthusiasts. Hiking, mountain biking, and climbing are popular activities.

The weather is generally warm and pleasant, with longer daylight hours, allowing you to explore the stunning alpine landscapes.

It's also a great time for paragliding and other adventure sports.

Autumn (September to November):

Autumn is a transitional period with cooler temperatures and fewer crowds.

The changing foliage creates a picturesque landscape, and hiking remains enjoyable in September.

If you prefer a quieter visit and don't mind the cooler evenings, this can be an excellent time to explore the region.

The best time to visit Chamonix depends on your interests. If you're into skiing and winter sports, winter is your season.

For a mix of outdoor activities and pleasant weather, consider summer.

Those who prefer milder weather and fewer crowds might find spring or autumn to be the perfect time to experience the beauty of Chamonix. Remember to check the specific weather conditions and resort openings before planning your trip, as they can vary from year to year.

When planning a trip to Chamonix, France, it's crucial to ensure you have the necessary visa and travel documents to make your journey smooth and hassle-free. Here's what you need to know:

Visa and Travel Documents

Passport: Ensure that your passport is valid for at least six months beyond your planned date of departure from Chamonix. Check its expiration date and renew it if necessary.

Visa: Chamonix is located in France, which is a member of the Schengen Agreement. Depending on your nationality, you may need a Schengen visa for short stays in Chamonix.

Check the French embassy or consulate website in your country to determine if you require a visa and the specific requirements for your application.

Travel Insurance: Consider purchasing comprehensive travel insurance that covers medical emergencies, trip cancellations, and lost luggage. It's a smart precaution to have coverage while traveling abroad.

Flight Tickets: Ensure that you have your flight tickets or electronic confirmations readily available for inspection when entering France.

Accommodation Confirmation: It's a good practice to carry printed or digital confirmation of your hotel reservations in Chamonix.

Travel Itinerary: Have a detailed itinerary of your trip, including transportation arrangements within Chamonix and any planned activities.

Currency: Bring some Euros with you for initial expenses. Chamonix is a popular tourist destination, and most places accept credit cards, but having some cash on hand is always useful.

Emergency Contacts: Carry a list of important phone numbers, including your country's embassy or consulate in France, local emergency numbers, and contacts for your travel insurance provider.

Health precautions

To ensure a safe and enjoyable trip, it's crucial to take health precautions:

Altitude Acclimatization:

Chamonix's high altitude can lead to altitude sickness. Spend a day or two at lower altitudes to acclimatize before engaging in strenuous activities.

Sun Protection:

The mountain sun can be intense. Pack sunscreen, sunglasses, and a wide-brimmed hat to shield yourself from UV rays.

Hydration:

High-altitude environments can cause dehydration. Drink plenty of water, especially if you're engaging in physical activities.

Weather-Appropriate Clothing:

Weather can change rapidly in the Alps. Dress in layers and bring waterproof clothing to stay comfortable in varying conditions.

Physical Fitness:

Some activities in Chamonix require good physical fitness. Prepare by exercising and consulting your doctor if necessary.

Insurance:

Ensure you have comprehensive travel insurance that covers medical emergencies and mountain rescue, as these services can be costly.

COVID-19 Precautions:

Stay updated on COVID-19 regulations and requirements. Bring masks, hand sanitizer, and follow local guidelines.

Vaccinations:

Check if any specific vaccinations are recommended before traveling to France or Chamonix.

Medications:

Carry any necessary medications and prescriptions with you. Familiarize yourself with local pharmacies and emergency medical facilities.

Emergency Numbers:

Save local emergency numbers, including those for mountain rescue and medical assistance, in your phone.

Chamonix Currency and Banking

Chamonix is a picturesque town located in the French Alps, and the primary currency used in Chamonix is the Euro (EUR, €).

Euros come in various denominations, including coins (1 cent, 2 cents, 5 cents, 10 cents, 20 cents, 50 cents, and 1 euro) and banknotes (5 euros, 10 euros, 20 euros, 50 euros, 100 euros, 200 euros, and 500 euros).

While the Euro is the official currency, Chamonix being a popular international tourist destination, also accepts other major currencies.

Many hotels, restaurants, and shops may accept US Dollars (USD), British Pounds (GBP), Swiss Francs (CHF), and sometimes even Japanese Yen (JPY) or Canadian Dollars

(CAD). However, it's important to note that exchange rates for these currencies may not be as favorable as using the Euro, and you may receive change in Euros.

Currency Exchange: Visitors arriving in Chamonix can exchange their home currency for Euros at various exchange offices, banks, and ATMs located throughout the town. Many hotels and businesses also accept major credit cards, such as Visa and MasterCard.

ATMs: Automated Teller Machines (ATMs) are readily available and accept international debit and credit cards. It's advisable to check with your bank regarding any foreign transaction fees that may apply when using ATMs abroad.

Banking Hours: Banks in Chamonix typically operate from Monday to Friday, with varying hours. Some may close for an extended lunch break, so it's advisable to plan your banking transactions accordingly.

Traveler's Checks: While less common today due to the convenience of ATMs, some establishments may still accept traveler's checks. However, they are not as widely used as credit and debit cards.

Currency Exchange Rates: Exchange rates can fluctuate, so it's a good idea to check rates at different exchange offices or banks to get the best value for your currency.

Banking Services: Chamonix offers a range of banking services, including currency exchange, international wire transfers, and assistance with financial matters. English-speaking staff can often be found at larger banks to assist tourists.

Mobile Banking: Mobile banking apps have gained popularity in recent years, making it easy to manage your finances on the go. Many banks in Chamonix offer mobile banking services for account holders.

Overall, Chamonix's currency and banking services are well-equipped to cater to the needs of both tourists and residents, ensuring a seamless financial experience during your stay in this picturesque Alpine town.

It's always a good idea to inform your bank of your travel plans to prevent any issues with your cards while abroad and to stay informed about any currency-related updates during your visit.

CHAPTER TWO

Chamonix Town Overview (Neighborhoods and Villages).

Chamonix-Mont-Blanc

This is the main hub and the town after which the whole valley is named.

Here, you'll discover a vibrant atmosphere with bustling streets filled with shops, restaurants, and cafes. The majestic Mont Blanc towers over the town, providing an awe-inspiring backdrop.

Argentière

Located a short drive or train ride north of Chamonix-Mont-Blanc, Argentière is famous for its proximity to the Grands Montets ski area.

It has a more relaxed ambiance and offers great opportunities for winter sports and hiking in the summer.

Les Houches

Known for its family-friendly atmosphere, Les Houches is located to the southwest of Chamonix-Mont-Blanc. It boasts beautiful scenery, excellent ski slopes, and a charming village center.

Vallorcine

This peaceful village, situated at the far end of the Chamonix Valley, is a haven for those seeking tranquility and natural beauty. It's an ideal starting point for hiking and exploring the Aiguilles Rouges Nature Reserve.

Le Tour

Nestled at the valley's northern tip, Le Tour is another fantastic spot for ski enthusiasts.

Its proximity to the Swiss border makes it a gateway to cross-border skiing adventures.

Les Bossons and Les Praz

These quaint neighborhoods offer a quieter alternative to Chamonix-Mont-Blanc while still providing access to the town's amenities. Les Praz is particularly charming with its traditional Savoyard architecture.

Servoz

Located at the valley's entrance, Servoz is a picturesque village with a peaceful vibe. It's an excellent base for exploring the Gorges de la Diosaz and enjoying leisurely walks.

Hidden Gems in Chamonix

Le Lac Blanc

A challenging hike or cable car ride away from the town, Le Lac Blanc offers a serene alpine lake surrounded by awe-inspiring peaks.

The panoramic views from here are simply breathtaking.

Le Chalet des Pyrénées

Tucked away from the bustling center, this charming restaurant offers authentic Savoyard cuisine in a cozy and traditional setting. It's a delightful culinary gem for food connoisseurs.

Montenvers Mer de Glace

Reachable by a vintage rack railway, this spot takes you to the largest glacier in France. Exploring the ice caves and witnessing the glacier's majestic expanse is a unique experience.

La Joux

This quaint hamlet is a short drive from Chamonix and is home to a serene forested area and a beautiful waterfall. It's a hidden gem for those seeking tranquility and a peaceful picnic spot.

Gorges de la Diosaz

Located a bit further from Chamonix, these stunning gorges offer a surreal natural spectacle with suspended walkways that wind through a lush, green canyon.

Café de l'Arve

A cozy café tucked away in the town, it's a perfect place to savor local pastries and a hot drink while watching the world go by.

Chamonix Bus Network

The primary mode of local transportation is the extensive bus network that connects the town center to various neighborhoods and attractions. The buses are clean, reliable, and offer a convenient way to move around the valley.

Chamonix Mont-Blanc Train Station

Chamonix has its own train station, making it accessible by rail from major French cities like Lyon and Paris. The Mont-Blanc Express train provides picturesque journeys between Chamonix and nearby Alpine destinations.

Cable Cars and Gondolas

Given its mountainous terrain, Chamonix relies heavily on cable cars and gondolas to transport visitors to the higher elevations, offering breathtaking views of Mont Blanc and the surrounding peaks.

Walking and Biking

The town is pedestrian-friendly, and walking or biking is a pleasant way to explore the streets, parks, and nearby trails. You can easily rent bicycles in the town.

Taxi and Rideshare

Taxis are available for those looking for a more private mode of transportation. Additionally, rideshare services like Uber operate in Chamonix.

Car Rentals

While not always necessary for getting around within Chamonix itself, renting a car can be useful if you plan to explore more remote areas of the region.

Cultures and Traditions of Chamonix

Alpine Heritage: Chamonix has a deep-rooted alpine heritage that revolves around mountaineering and winter sports. It's known as the "Capital of Extreme Sports" and has a strong mountaineering history dating back to the 18th century when explorers and climbers began tackling the challenging peaks of the Mont Blanc massif.

Traditional Architecture: Chamonix boasts charming alpine architecture with wooden chalets adorned with intricate carvings and flower-filled balconies.

These buildings reflect the region's history and blend seamlessly with the natural surroundings.

Festivals and Events: The town hosts various cultural festivals and events throughout the year, celebrating music, art, and mountain culture. The Musilac Mont-Blanc music festival and the Chamonix Adventure Festival are popular annual gatherings.

Cuisine: Savoyard cuisine dominates Chamonix's dining scene. Traditional dishes like fondue, raclette, tartiflette, and diots (sausages) are commonly enjoyed in cozy mountain restaurants. Local cheeses, such as Beaufort and Reblochon, are also culinary staples.

Music and Dance: Traditional Alpine music and dance performances are occasionally showcased, featuring accordion music and traditional folk dances. These events offer visitors a glimpse into the local culture.

Sports: Skiing and snowboarding are central to Chamonix's culture, with the town hosting international winter sports competitions like the Freeride World Tour. The Alpine Museum in Chamonix is a great place to learn more about the history of mountaineering and winter sports in the region.

Art and Craft: Chamonix has a thriving arts and crafts scene, with local artisans producing handcrafted goods like pottery, jewelry, and woodwork. You can find unique souvenirs that reflect the region's culture and craftsmanship.

Language: While French is the official language, English is widely spoken in Chamonix due to its popularity as an international tourist destination.

Basic Communication in Chamonix

Bonjour - Hello

Bonsoir - Good evening

Bonne nuit - Good night

Salut - Hi

Comment ça va ? - How are you?

Ça va bien, merci - I'm fine, thank you.

Quel est votre nom ? - What's your name?

Je m'appelle [votre nom] - My name is [your name].

S'il vous plaît - Please

Merci - Thank you

De rien - You're welcome

Excusez-moi - Excuse me

Oui - Yes

Non - No

Parlez-vous anglais ? - Do you speak English?

Je ne parle pas bien le français - I don't speak French well.

Pouvez-vous m'aider ? - Can you help me?

Où est... ? - Where is...?

Combien ça coûte ? - How much does it cost?

L'addition, s'il vous plaît - The check, please

Je voudrais... - I would like...

Pouvez-vous me recommander un restaurant ? - Can you recommend a restaurant?

Je suis perdu(e) - I am lost

J'ai besoin d'une ambulance - I need an ambulance

Où sont les toilettes ? - Where are the restrooms?

Je ne comprends pas - I don't understand

Aidez-moi - Help me

Je suis allergique à... - I am allergic to...

J'ai une réservation - I have a reservation

Au revoir – Goodbye

The Chamonix Cuisine

Savoyard Specialties: Savoyard cuisine is at the heart of Chamonix's culinary identity. Fondue and raclette, both featuring melted cheese, are beloved dishes. In a cozy mountain restaurant, you can dip bread, potatoes, and charcuterie into a pot of warm, gooey cheese.

Tartiflette: Another iconic dish is tartiflette, made with potatoes, reblochon cheese, lardons (bacon bits), and onions. It's a hearty and indulgent treat, perfect for replenishing energy after a day on the slopes.

Fresh Alpine Ingredients: Chamonix cuisine takes advantage of the region's natural resources. You'll find fresh mountain trout, wild game, and mushrooms incorporated into various dishes, offering a taste of the Alpine wilderness.

Haute Cuisine: Chamonix also boasts a selection of high-end restaurants, some of which have earned Michelin stars. These establishments offer innovative takes on classic French cuisine, often featuring locally sourced ingredients.

Mountain-side Dining: Many restaurants in Chamonix offer picturesque mountain-side dining. Enjoy your meal while gazing at the breathtaking alpine scenery, creating a dining experience like no other.

International Flavors: Chamonix's international atmosphere is reflected in its diverse culinary scene. You can savor Italian, Swiss, and international cuisines alongside traditional French dishes.

Desserts and Pastries: Don't forget to indulge in Chamonix's delightful desserts and pastries. Try a slice of tarte aux myrtilles (blueberry tart) or a pain d'épices (spiced bread) for a sweet Alpine treat.

Accomodation Choices in Chamonix

Luxury Hotels: Chamonix boasts several high-end hotels with stunning mountain views, spa facilities, gourmet dining, and personalized service. These are perfect for travelers who seek a lavish experience.

Boutique Hotels: For a unique and charming stay, boutique hotels in Chamonix provide a blend of style and comfort. They often have distinctive designs and offer a more intimate atmosphere.

Ski-In/Ski-Out Chalets: If you're hitting the slopes, consider staying in a ski-in/ski-out chalet or apartment. These provide convenient access to the ski areas and are excellent for winter sports enthusiasts.

Traditional Alpine Chalets: Experience the quintessential alpine charm by renting a traditional chalet. These cozy accommodations often come with fireplaces and picturesque mountain views.

Budget Accommodations: Chamonix also offers budget-friendly options, including hostels and guesthouses. These are ideal for backpackers and those looking to minimize expenses while still enjoying the natural beauty of the region.

Vacation Rentals: Apartments and vacation homes are readily available, offering more space and the flexibility to cook your meals, making them suitable for families or longer stays.

Camping: If you're an outdoor enthusiast, Chamonix has campsites that allow you to experience the pristine beauty of the Alps up close.

When choosing your accommodation in Chamonix, consider the season of your visit, your preferred activities, and the level of comfort you desire. Regardless of your choice, you're sure to be surrounded by the breathtaking scenery and outdoor adventures that make Chamonix a sought-after destination in the French Alps.

Luxury Hotels in Chamonix

Hôtel Mont-Blanc Chamonix

Address: 62, allée du Majestic, Chamonix City Centre, 74400 Chamonix-Mont-Blanc, France

Nestled in the heart of Chamonix amidst a charming garden, Hotel Mont-Blanc offers elegant and refined accommodations. The hotel boasts picturesque mountain vistas and is home to an array of amenities, including a restaurant, bar, and a spa featuring a heated pool and an outdoor hot tub.

The rooms at Hotel Mont Blanc are thoughtfully adorned, each showcasing stunning mountain panoramas. They come complete with a flat-screen satellite TV and an iPod docking station. The en suite bathrooms offer a choice of bath or shower, and guests are provided with plush bathrobes, comfortable slippers, and complimentary toiletries.

For those seeking a hearty start to the day, Hotel Mont Blanc serves a delectable buffet breakfast daily, available for an additional fee.

In the evenings, guests can indulge in modern French cuisine at the on-site restaurant or unwind with a glass of wine or champagne in the bar.

Complimentary shuttle service to the ski slopes is at your disposal, and you'll find an ice rink and a cinema conveniently located nearby. Additionally, Chamonix Golf Course is just a brief 4-minute drive away.

Most popular facilities, Shuttle service (free), Skiing, Spa and wellness centre, Massage, Concierge service, Snack bar, Heating, Pets allowed, Fitness centre, Outdoor swimming pool

Le Hameau Albert 1er

Address: 38, Route du Bouchet, Chamonix City Centre, 74400 Chamonix-Mont-Blanc, France

Situated in the picturesque setting of Chamonix Mont-Blanc, this hotel boasts a complimentary shuttle service to the nearby ski slopes, making it an ideal choice for winter enthusiasts.

The establishment features both indoor and outdoor pools, a spa and wellness center, and complimentary Wi-Fi to enhance your stay. The property is comprised of two distinct buildings: L'Albert 1er and La Ferme.

Every snug room at Le Hameau Albert 1er comes complete with a private bathroom, satellite TV, as well as plush bathrobes and comfortable slippers.

Culinary delights await at the hotel, with options ranging from a gourmet restaurant serving traditional cuisine to another offering authentic Savoyard specialties. Additionally, a well-stocked wine cellar and a stylish bar are at your disposal.

The wellness center is a haven of relaxation, featuring amenities such as a hammam, hot tub, sauna, and a variety of rejuvenating massage and body treatments.

Conveniently located just a brief 5-minute stroll from Chamonix SNCF train station, the hotel also provides complimentary private parking for your convenience.

Most popular facilities, Airport shuttle, Spa facilities, Massage, Skiing, Room service, Lift, 2 restaurants, Indoor swimming pool, Garden, Balcony

Auberge du Bois Prin

Address: 69 Chemin de l'Hermine, Chamonix City Centre, 74400 Chamonix-Mont-Blanc, France

Auberge du Bois Prin is conveniently situated just 500 meters, approximately a 15-minute stroll from Chamonix's city center and a mere 300 meters from the Le Brévent Ski Lift.

Our charming establishment boasts well-appointed en-suite guestrooms featuring complimentary Wi-Fi access, cable TV, and a balcony or garden view overlooking the stunning Mont Blanc mountain range.

For those seeking relaxation, we offer massages upon request for an additional fee.

Start your day with a delightful buffet breakfast, complete with homemade jams, served either on our terrace or in the dining room.

During the winter season, guests at Auberge du Bois Prin can partake in thrilling skiing and snowboarding on Chamonix's slopes. We also offer a convenient shuttle service to both the ski slopes and the city center upon reservation. Additionally, our hotel can assist in arranging ski passes and equipment rentals.

In the summertime, guests can indulge in hiking, horseback riding, and various watersports activities. Our location is also conveniently close to Chamonix Golf Course, just 4 km away.

Most popular facilities,Room service, Skiing, Wine/champagne, Concierge service, Pets allowed, Hiking, Restaurant, Terrace, Garden, Balcony

Les Grands Montets Hotel & Spa

Address: 340, Chemin des Arbérons, Argentière, 74400 Chamonix-Mont-Blanc, France

This charming chalet is nestled beneath the renowned Grands Montets ski area, serving as the perfect launchpad for various hiking trails.

Its generously appointed rooms, some of which feature mezzanines for families, offer captivating vistas of either Mont-Blanc or the Argentière Glacier.

Exuding the quintessential chalet style, these rooms and suites provide inviting and well-lit living spaces.

Each boasts a balcony, individual heating, a television, and private bathrooms equipped with both a bath and shower.

Les Grands Montets Hotel & Spa takes care of your post-skiing needs, offering an indoor swimming pool, an outdoor hot tub, a sauna, fitness facilities, and a steam room. You can also indulge in rejuvenating massages upon request.

During the winter, cozy up by the bar's fireplace with a drink or enjoy a game of billiards. In the summer, relish the expansive terrace adorned with sunbeds, gazing out towards Mont Blanc.

Wi-Fi connectivity is accessible in the common areas of Les Grands Montets Hotel & Spa, and complimentary parking is readily available on-site.

Additionally, throughout the year, the hotel provides ski lockers, shoe dryers, and multi-passes for your convenience.

Most popular facilities, Spa facilities, Massage, Hot tub, Skiing, Sauna

Lockers, Snack bar, 24-hour front desk, Concierge service, Hiking.

Grand Hôtel des Alpes

Address: 75, rue du Docteur Paccard, Chamonix City Centre, 74400 Chamonix-Mont-Blanc, France

Nestled in the picturesque town of Chamonix, at the base of Mont Blanc and amidst the breathtaking Alpine mountains, the Grand Hotel des Alpes offers a truly distinctive lodging experience. Guests enjoy access to an extensive DVD collection spanning various languages, a secure private garage, and a dedicated ski room complete with a convenient shoe dryer.

The staffs are warm and attentive and will welcomes you with grace, creating an ambiance that exudes both elegance and familiarity. Savor the tasteful wooden decor, unwind in the cozy lounge overlooking the majestic Massif de Mont Blanc, or relax by the fireplace in our inviting bar.

The guestrooms are thoughtfully designed, radiating warmth and style. Each one is equipped with modern en suite amenities, satellite TV, and complimentary Wi-Fi for your convenience.

This charming location provides the perfect vantage point to relish the town's quintessential charm year-round, along with the enchanting natural beauty that surrounds it.

As an added benefit, our property offers ski pass sales and a complimentary winter shuttle service to the Chamonix ski slopes upon request. The Grand Hotel des Alpes also facilitates guided mountain excursions and ski instructor sessions, making your Alpine adventures even more accessible.

Conveniently located just 650 meters from the Aiguille du Midi cable car, our hotel ensures easy access to unforgettable mountain experiences. We invite you to book your stay with us and embark on a memorable Chamonix journey.

Most popular facilities, Spa facilities, Skiing, Massage, Room service, Concierge service, Airport shuttle, Superb breakfast, Sauna, Board games/puzzles, Steam room.

Affordable Hotels in Chamonix

Cosmiques Hotel - Centre Chamonix

Address: 37 impasse des Rhododendrons, Chamonix City Centre, 74400 Chamonix-Mont-Blanc, France

Cosmiques Hotel - Centre Chamonix in Chamonix-Mont-Blanc offers an array of amenities and services for its guests. This charming establishment boasts a shared lounge and terrace, a restaurant, and a bar, creating a comfortable and welcoming atmosphere.

Situated approximately 20 km from Skyway Monte Bianco, 9.3 km from Aiguille du Midi, and 9.4 km from Step into the Void, the hotel's location is ideal for exploring the surrounding natural wonders.

For guests' convenience, the hotel provides ski storage facilities. Each room at the hotel features a private bathroom with a shower and complimentary toiletries, as well as free WiFi to keep you connected during your stay.

Start your day with a delicious breakfast, with options ranging from continental to vegetarian or gluten-free, served daily at the property.

Those staying at Cosmiques Hotel - Centre Chamonix can partake in various activities in the Chamonix-Mont-Blanc area, including skiing.

The multilingual reception staff, fluent in English, Spanish, and French, are available to assist guests with information and recommendations.

Notable attractions nearby include Montenvers - Mer de Glace Train Station, Crystal Museum Chamonix, and Chamonix Casino.

The closest airport is Geneva International Airport, located 88 km from Cosmiques Hotel - Centre Chamonix.

Most popular facilities, Skiing, Bar, Heating, Pets allowed, Free WiFi, Good breakfast, Shared lounge/TV area, Restaurant, Soundproof rooms, 24-hour front desk

Langley Hotel Gustavia

Address: 272 Avenue Michel Croz, Chamonix City Centre, 74400 Chamonix-Mont-Blanc, France

Nestled in the heart of Chamonix, with stunning Mont Blanc as its backdrop, Hotel Gustavia boasts a rich history dating back to 1890.

Langley Hotel Gustavia's charming establishment offers a delightful array of amenities, including the inviting Chambre 9 bar, a picturesque terrace affording breathtaking Mont Blanc vistas, a cozy lounge with a fireplace, and complimentary Wi-Fi in the lobby.

Guest rooms are adorned with flat-screen TVs and showcase captivating mountain panoramas. Each room is equipped with a private bathroom, while select accommodations feature balconies, available upon request and subject to availability.

At Hotel Gustavia, we take pride in our individually decorated guest rooms. Additional offerings encompass a 24-hour reception desk, and we provide a free private parking area with limited availability, offering ten spaces for our guests.

Our restaurant presents a delectable breakfast buffet, and for lunch, a diverse selection of meals awaits. In the evening, indulge in classical international cuisine or explore our à la carte menu at Brasserie Chambre 9. The town center, replete with shops and restaurants, is a short stroll away.

Conveniently, a free shuttle service, located 500 meters from the hotel, provides transportation to the mountains. Hotel Gustavia stands opposite Chamonix Train Station and is a mere 15-minute drive from the Italian border. Geneva International Airport is located 99 km from our welcoming establishment.

Most popular facilities, Skiing, Heating, Hiking, Bar, Lift, Good breakfast, Massage, Board games/puzzles, Wine/champagne, Balcony

Vert Lodge Chamonix

Address: 964 Route des Gaillands, 74400 Chamonix-Mont-Blanc, France

Vert Lodge, a historic gem in Chamonix, boasts a prime location adjacent to Gaillands Lake and Climbing Wall, a mere 15-minute stroll from the town center. Ample public and private parking options are at your disposal.

Following a complete refurbishment in January 2021, our guest rooms are equipped with USB plugs, a television, ample storage, and private bathrooms. For those seeking a communal experience, we also offer shared dorms and capsule beds.

Vert Lodge's establishment features a spacious bar complete with a pool table and a restaurant offering a diverse international menu, with half-board options to cater to your culinary preferences.

Outside, you'll find our expansive garden area, perfect for relaxation, featuring plenty of seating and even a hammock. Our attentive staff is eager to assist with any inquiries or advice you may need, and you can conveniently obtain lift tickets and rental equipment on-site.

With a bus stop right outside the hotel and Pelerins SNCF Train Station just 300 meters away, accessibility is a breeze. Geneva Airport is a little over an hour's drive away, making

Vert Lodge the ideal starting point for your Chamonix adventure.

Most popular facilities, Live sport events (broadcast), Skiing, Hiking, Bar, Board games/puzzles, Snack bar, Restaurant, Wine/champagne, Bicycle rental, Breakfast

Wanderlust Hotel Chamonix

Address: 59 Route vers le Nant, Les Bossons, 74400 Chamonix-Mont-Blanc, France

Nestled within an alpine garden at the base of the majestic Bossons Glacier, Wanderlust Motels Chamonix presents an array of enticing amenities. Among them, you'll find a heated indoor pool and a relaxing hot tub, perfect for unwinding after a day of adventure.

A convenient public shuttle service is at your disposal, ready to transport you to Chamonix's center, just 4.5 km away. Furthermore, you'll appreciate the availability of complimentary parking during your stay.

The air-conditioned guest rooms at Wanderlust Motels Chamonix are thoughtfully equipped with a flat-screen TV featuring satellite channels and a private bathroom. Some rooms offer picturesque mountain vistas.

Start your day with a satisfying buffet breakfast to fuel your adventures.

The hotel boasts a 24-hour reception and offers additional amenities like ski storage and a children's play area complete with board games. For golf enthusiasts, Chamonix Golf Club is a mere 15-minute drive away.

Wandercoffee, open 24/7, invites you to immerse yourself in the lively pop and folk atmosphere of its communal spaces. Gather here for delightful treats like a delectable chocolate muffin paired with a steaming cup of coffee. Each evening, the temptation of savoring the homemade dish of the day or indulging in one of our scrumptious mountain specialties is sure to bring smiles to all.

Most popular facilities, Games room, Table tennis, Kids' club, Board games/puzzles, Skiing, Shared lounge/TV area, Toilet with grab rails, Indoor swimming pool, Hiking, Wine/champagne

Beautiful cosy, modern studio in Chamonix centre

Address: 555 Route Couttet Champion, Chamonix City Centre, 74400 Chamonix-Mont-Blanc, France

Nestled in the heart of Chamonix-Mont-Blanc's city center, you'll find this charming, contemporary studio apartment. It's perfectly located, just 19 km away from Skyway Monte Bianco, 1.3 km from Montenvers - Mer de Glace Train Station, and 8.8 km from Aiguille du Midi. Plus, the convenience of free private parking and an elevator awaits you here.

Inside, this one-bedroom apartment offers complimentary WiFi, a flat-screen TV, and a well-equipped kitchen with a microwave and refrigerator. You'll also find plush towels and crisp bed linen provided for your comfort.

When it comes to local attractions, Step Into the Void is a mere 8.9 km away, and the captivating Crystal Museum Chamonix is just 1.2 km from your doorstep.

The Geneva International Airport, your gateway to this lovely studio in Chamonix center, is conveniently located 87 km away.

Most popular facilities, Free parking, Free WiFi, Pets allowed, Lift

CHAPTER THREE

Exploring Chamonix

Exploring Chamonix is like embarking on a journey into an alpine wonderland that captivates the senses at every turn.

Nestled in the French Alps, this charming town is a haven for outdoor enthusiasts and nature lovers.

From the towering peaks of Mont Blanc to the pristine glacial valleys, Chamonix's breathtaking landscapes offer a playground for hikers, climbers, skiers, and adventurers of all kinds.

The Aiguille du Midi cable car provides a thrilling ride to the heart of the mountains, offering panoramic views that will leave you in awe.

In addition, to its natural beauty, Chamonix boasts a vibrant town center with quaint streets lined with cafes, shops, and cozy chalets. The alpine cuisine is a treat for the taste buds, with fondue and raclette being local favorites.

Exploring Chamonix is not just an outdoor escapade; it's an immersion into the alpine culture, a chance to conquer nature's challenges, and a gateway to forging unforgettable memories in the heart of the French Alps.

The Majestic Mont Blanc: Europe's Tallest Peak

Mont Blanc, standing proudly at 4,808.7 meters (15,777 feet) above sea level, reigns supreme as the tallest mountain in Europe.

Nestled within the breathtaking French Alps, this majestic peak has captivated the imagination of adventurers, mountaineers, and nature enthusiasts for centuries.

Its awe-inspiring stature, draped in glistening glaciers, exudes an aura of grandeur and mystery. Mont Blanc, aptly named the "White Mountain," is a testament to the Earth's formidable geological forces.

For mountaineers, the challenge of scaling Mont Blanc is a lifelong aspiration, with its steep slopes and unpredictable weather presenting a formidable test of skill and determination.

The reward, however, is unparalleled: panoramic vistas of pristine alpine landscapes that extend for miles in every direction.

Beyond the thrill of mountaineering, Mont Blanc offers an array of outdoor activities year-round, from skiing in the winter to hiking and paragliding in the summer. The charming alpine towns that dot the region provide a cozy retreat after a day of exploration.

Whether you're an adventurer seeking to conquer its heights or simply an admirer of natural wonders, Mont Blanc stands as a symbol of Europe's untamed beauty and a testament to the enduring allure of the mountains.

Chamonix Town: A Hub of Activity and Charm

Nestled in the heart of the French Alps, Chamonix Town stands as a vibrant hub of activity and charm, beckoning adventurers, nature lovers, and culture enthusiasts alike.

This picturesque mountain town is renowned for its breathtaking vistas of Mont Blanc, the highest peak in Western Europe, which dominates the horizon and sets the stage for unforgettable experiences.

Chamonix is a playground for outdoor enthusiasts, offering world-class skiing and snowboarding in the winter, and hiking, mountain biking, and paragliding during the summer months.

The bustling town center exudes a delightful Alpine charm, with quaint cafes, boutique shops, and cozy chalets lining its cobbled streets.

Beyond the stunning natural beauty and adrenaline-pumping activities, Chamonix also boasts a rich cultural heritage.

The town hosts various events, from music festivals to art exhibitions, showcasing its dynamic arts scene.

"Adventures in the Alps: Skiing, Hiking, and More

The majestic Alps, Europe's most iconic mountain range, beckon adventurers to experience the thrill of a lifetime. Nestled amidst the rugged peaks and picturesque valleys, the Alps offer an array of exhilarating activities for nature enthusiasts and adrenaline junkies alike.

Skiing: The Alps are a winter wonderland, boasting world-class ski resorts like Chamonix, Zermatt, and St. Anton. Whether you're a seasoned skier or a novice hitting the slopes for the first time, the Alps offer a variety of terrain to suit all levels. The sensation of gliding down pristine slopes surrounded by breathtaking vistas is an experience like no other.

Hiking: During the summer months, the Alps transform into a hiker's paradise. Countless trails meander through alpine meadows, dense forests, and alongside glistening lakes. Whether you're embarking on a challenging multi-day trek or a leisurely day hike, the beauty of the Alps unfolds at every step.

Beyond skiing and hiking, the Alps offer a range of adventures, including mountain biking, paragliding, and rock climbing. Explore charming alpine villages, savor delectable cuisine, and immerse yourself in the rich cultural heritage of the region.

Adventures in the Alps are a blend of adrenaline, natural beauty, and cultural discovery, making it a destination that leaves an indelible mark on the hearts of all who venture here.

Must-See Attractions and Activitie

Tahiti boasts a plethora of must-see attractions and activities that promise to captivate every traveler's heart. Here are some of the highlights:

Matira Beach

Nestled on the island of Bora Bora, Matira Beach is a paradise on Earth. Its powdery white sands, crystal-clear waters, and stunning sunsets make it a romantic haven and a must-visit spot.

Snorkeling and Diving

Explore the vibrant marine life in Tahiti's pristine waters. From swimming alongside sharks and rays in Bora Bora's lagoon to discovering colorful coral gardens, the underwater world is a treasure trove for divers and snorkelers.

Waterfalls and Hiking

Tahiti's lush interior is adorned with picturesque waterfalls and hiking trails. Don't miss the opportunity to trek through the verdant forests to discover hidden gems like the Fautaua Waterfall.

Tahitian Culture

Immerse yourself in Polynesian culture by attending traditional dance performances, exploring archaeological sites, and indulging in local cuisine at an authentic Tahitian feast.

Pearl Farms

Tahiti is famous for its exquisite black pearls. Take a tour of a pearl farm to learn about the pearl cultivation process and perhaps acquire a unique souvenir.

Circle Island Tou

Explore the islands via a scenic circle island tour. These guided excursions offer a comprehensive view of the landscape, culture, and history of Tahiti.

Vanilla Plantations

Visit a vanilla plantation to witness the cultivation of one of Tahiti's prized exports. Learn about the pollination process and purchase some high-quality vanilla products.

Shark and Ray Feeding

Get up close and personal with blacktip reef sharks and stingrays during guided feeding excursions in the lagoons. It's an exhilarating and educational experience.

Sunset Cruises

Indulge in a romantic sunset cruise on the calm waters of Tahiti. Sip tropical cocktails, enjoy a traditional Polynesian dance show, and witness the sun setting over the horizon.

Brevent-Flegere

Explore this hiking and skiing area offering panoramic vistas, accessible by cable car. It's particularly stunning during the fall foliage season.

Les Granges d'en Haut

Discover a traditional alpine farm and learn about mountain life in the region.

You can even enjoy a delicious Savoyard meal here.

Gorges de la Diosaz

A short drive from Chamonix, these impressive natural gorges offer a unique perspective of the region's geology.

Cosmiques Ridge

For experienced climbers, this challenging ridge offers an exciting ascent with incredible views.

CHAPTER FOUR

Things to Do in Chamonix

Mont Blanc

The crown jewel of Chamonix, Mont Blanc is Western Europe's highest peak.

Whether you're an experienced mountaineer or a casual hiker, there are numerous trails and cable cars to take you closer to this iconic mountain.

Aiguille du Midi

Take a cable car ride to Aiguille du Midi for breathtaking panoramic views of Mont Blanc and the surrounding peaks. It's a fantastic vantage point and offers a unique perspective on the mountains.

Mer de Glace

Visit the "Sea of Ice," one of the largest glaciers in Europe. A cogwheel train takes you to the glacier's edge, where you can explore ice caves and learn about the glacier's history.

Hiking and Trekking

Chamonix offers a vast network of hiking and trekking trails for all levels of hikers.

From leisurely strolls to challenging multi-day treks, there's something for everyone.

Skiing and Snowboarding

In the winter, Chamonix is a mecca for skiers and snowboarders, with world-class slopes and resorts like Les Granges and Brevent-Flegere.

Adventure Sports

For adrenaline junkies, try paragliding, rock climbing, canyoning, or white-water rafting.

Chamonix Town

Stroll through the charming town center, lined with shops, restaurants, and cafes. Explore its Alpine architecture and immerse yourself in the local culture.

Alpine Museums

Learn about the history and culture of Chamonix's mountaineering heritage at the Alpine Museum and the Crystal Museum.

Day Trips

Take day trips to nearby attractions like Annecy, Geneva, or the picturesque villages of the Mont Blanc region.

Relaxation

Don't forget to unwind in Chamonix's spas and wellness centers after a day of adventure.

Beaches to Visit in Chamonix

Chamonix, renowned for its spectacular mountain scenery and world-class skiing, also offers a surprising gem for beach enthusiasts: serene alpine beaches.

While it may not boast sandy shores typical of tropical destinations, Chamonix's unique beaches provide a tranquil and picturesque setting for relaxation.

Here are some notable Chamonix beaches to consider during your visit:

Lac des Gaillands

Nestled at the foot of the Aiguilles Rouges, this crystal-clear lake offers a peaceful beach area with stunning mountain views.

Enjoy a refreshing swim in the chilly waters, try paddleboarding, or simply sunbathe on the pebble shore.

Lac de Passy

Located a short drive from Chamonix, this picturesque lake features a sandy beach, making it a popular spot for families.

It's perfect for swimming, picnicking, and taking in the beautiful surroundings.

Lac Blanc

For a more adventurous beach experience, consider hiking to Lac Blanc.

This pristine mountain lake offers awe-inspiring vistas of Mont Blanc and the surrounding peaks.

Although swimming is possible, the water is chilly even in summer.

Plan d'Eau Biotope

Situated in the heart of Chamonix, this biotope lake is surrounded by greenery and offers a designated swimming area with a sandy beach.

It's a fantastic spot to cool off on a hot summer day.

Les Granges

Located along the Arve River, this peaceful riverside beach is a great place to relax and unwind. The clear waters and scenic views provide a tranquil escape from the hustle and bustle of town.

Sporting Activities in Chamoix

Skiing and Snowboarding: Chamonix is a winter sports paradise with access to multiple ski areas, including the famous Mont Blanc.

Skiers and snowboarders of all levels can enjoy the pristine slopes, deep powder, and challenging terrain.

Mountaineering

Known as the "Capital of Extreme Sports," Chamonix attracts mountaineers from around the world. Scaling Mont Blanc, the highest peak in Western Europe, is a pinnacle achievement for many adventurers.

Hiking and Trekking

During the warmer months, Chamonix offers an extensive network of hiking and trekking trails.

The breathtaking landscapes, including lush valleys and glaciers, make it an ideal destination for outdoor enthusiasts.

Climbing

The region boasts excellent rock climbing opportunities. Climbers can test their skills on natural cliffs or indoor climbing walls.

Paragliding

Soar above the mountains and valleys for a bird's-eye view of Chamonix. Paragliding offers an exhilarating experience and breathtaking scenery.

Mountain Biking

Chamonix offers an extensive network of mountain biking trails, from leisurely rides to challenging downhill courses.

Golf

The Chamonix Golf Club provides a unique golfing experience with stunning mountain views as a backdrop.

Ice Climbing

In the winter, ice climbing enthusiasts can tackle frozen waterfalls and ice-covered cliffs in the surrounding areas.

Trail Running

Chamonix hosts the iconic Ultra-Trail du Mont-Blanc (UTMB) race, attracting elite trail runners from around the globe.

The town is also a hotspot for trail running enthusiasts with various routes catering to different fitness levels.

White-Water Sports

Nearby rivers offer opportunities for white-water rafting and kayaking, providing an adrenaline rush against the backdrop of the alpine landscape.

Spas and Wellness Centers

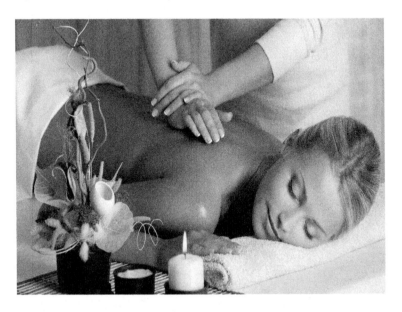

Thermes de Saint-Gervais: Just a short drive from Chamonix, the Thermes de Saint-Gervais is a thermal spa where you can immerse yourself in the healing properties of natural thermal waters.

The spa offers a range of treatments, including hydrotherapy, massages, and facials, all set against a backdrop of breathtaking mountain vistas.

Les Granges d'en Haut Spa

Located in a luxurious chalet, Les Granges d'en Haut Spa offers a serene environment for indulging in massages, body treatments, and holistic therapies.

Their skilled therapists ensure you leave feeling completely relaxed and rejuvenated.

QC Terme Chamonix

Situated in the heart of Chamonix, QC Terme offers a modern and tranquil setting with thermal baths, saunas, steam rooms, and a wide variety of wellness treatments. It's a perfect place to unwind after a day on the slopes.

Deep Nature Spa

Found within the luxurious Hôtel Mont-Blanc, Deep Nature Spa offers a range of spa treatments and an inviting pool area. It's an excellent choice for those seeking a serene and upscale spa experience.

Le Bachal Spa

Tucked away in Les Granges d'en Haut, Le Bachal Spa combines traditional and contemporary techniques to provide a range of treatments, including massages, facials, and body scrubs.

The serene atmosphere and skilled therapists make it a top choice for relaxation.

Yoga and Meditation Retreats

Chamonix, known for its breathtaking alpine scenery and serene ambiance, is an ideal destination for those seeking solace and spiritual rejuvenation through yoga and meditation retreats.

Nestled amidst the French Alps, this picturesque town offers a tranquil backdrop that perfectly complements the practice of mindfulness and self-discovery.

Yoga and meditation retreats in Chamonix provide participants with a unique opportunity to connect with nature while delving deep into their inner selves.

Imagine practicing yoga poses at the foothills of majestic mountains, breathing in the pure mountain air, and meditating by serene alpine lakes.

These retreats often feature experienced instructors who guide participants through various yoga styles and meditation techniques, catering to all levels of expertise.

It's a chance to disconnect from the stresses of daily life, embrace holistic well-being, and embark on a transformative journey towards inner peace and balance.

Many retreats in Chamonix offer customizable packages that include not only yoga and meditation sessions but also outdoor adventures like hiking, skiing, and spa treatments for a holistic wellness experience.

Whether you're a seasoned yogi or a novice looking to start your mindfulness journey, Chamonix's yoga and meditation retreats are a gateway to self-discovery and profound relaxation in one of the world's most stunning natural settings.

So, if you seek to harmonize your mind, body, and spirit amidst the grandeur of the Alps, Chamonix beckons as a sanctuary for your inner exploration.

Thermal Baths

Nestled amidst the stunning French Alps, Chamonix is renowned for its picturesque landscapes and world-class outdoor activities.

However, beyond its famous ski slopes and hiking trails, Chamonix also offers a tranquil and rejuvenating experience at its thermal baths.

Chamonix's thermal baths provide the perfect contrast to the adrenaline-packed adventures of the region. These natural, geothermal hot springs are rich in minerals, known for their therapeutic properties, and have been enjoyed for centuries by locals and travelers alike.

The soothing, warm waters have a calming effect on tired muscles, making them ideal for après-ski relaxation or post-hike recovery.

One of the most popular thermal baths in Chamonix is the "Les Granges" complex, which features indoor and outdoor pools, saunas, steam rooms, and relaxation areas with breathtaking mountain views.

It's a serene oasis where you can unwind and let the healing waters melt away any stress or fatigue.

Smartphone and Camera Tips for Capturing Chamonix's Beauty

Golden Hours: Chamonix boasts breathtaking scenery, and the best time to capture it is during the "golden hours" just after sunrise and before sunset. The soft, warm light during these times enhances the mountainous landscapes.

Wide Angle Lens: If you have a camera with interchangeable lenses, a wide-angle lens is a must.

It allows you to capture the vastness of Chamonix's valleys and mountains.

Use Filters: Polarizing filters can help reduce glare from snow and water, making your photos more vibrant. Neutral density filters are useful for long-exposure shots of waterfalls and rivers.

Stabilize Your Shots: Chamonix's terrain can be rugged, so use a tripod or a stable surface to prevent shaky shots, especially in low light.

Capture the Action: Chamonix is a hub for outdoor activities. Capture the excitement of skiing, mountaineering, or paragliding by using burst mode or sports settings on your camera.

HDR Mode: High Dynamic Range (HDR) mode on smartphones can help balance the contrast between bright skies and shaded landscapes, producing more detailed photos.

Local Flora and Fauna: Don't forget to capture the unique alpine flora and wildlife. Keep a safe distance and use a telephoto lens or zoom on your smartphone to avoid disturbing animals.

Panoramas: Chamonix offers sweeping vistas. Use the panorama mode on your smartphone or take a series of photos to create stunning panoramic views.

Night Photography: Capture the starry skies or the town's illuminated streets at night. Use a tripod and a slow shutter speed to achieve beautiful night shots.

Editing: Post-processing can enhance your photos. Use photo editing apps or software to adjust exposure, contrast, and color balance to make your images truly pop.

CONCLUSION

In conclusion, a visit to Chamonix is an extraordinary journey that combines the awe-inspiring grandeur of the French Alps with the charm of an alpine village. Whether you're a passionate skier, a nature enthusiast, or simply seeking a serene mountain escape, Chamonix has something to offer every traveler.

The dramatic peaks, cascading glaciers, and endless outdoor adventures make Chamonix a haven for thrill-seekers and nature lovers alike. The town's quaint streets, lined with cozy cafes and charming shops, provide the perfect backdrop for leisurely strolls and cultural immersion.

Chamonix's rich history as a mountaineering hub adds a layer of allure to this already captivating destination. The spirit of adventure and exploration is palpable in the air, inspiring all who visit.

As you bid adieu to Chamonix, you'll carry with you not only memories of breathtaking vistas but also a sense of exhilaration and connection to the natural world. Chamonix is more than a destination; it's an invitation to embrace the majesty of the mountains and create lasting memories in one of the world's most captivating alpine retreats.

Printed in Great Britain
by Amazon

37171452R00059